USDA

United States
Department of
Agriculture

Forest Service

Pacific Northwest
Research Station

General Technical Report
PNW-GTR-819

July 2010

Timber Volume and Aboveground Live Tree Biomass Estimations for Landscape Analyses in the Pacific Northwest

Xiaoping Zhou and Miles A. Hemstrom

Authors

Xiaoping Zhou is a forester and **Miles A. Hemstrom** is a research ecologist, Forestry Sciences Laboratory, P.O. Box 3890, Portland, OR 97208-3890.

Abstract

Zhou, Xiaoping; Hemstrom, Miles A. 2010. Timber volume and aboveground live tree biomass estimations for landscape analyses in the Pacific Northwest. Gen. Tech. Rep. PNW-GTR-819. Portland, OR: U.S. Department of Agriculture, Forest Service, Pacific Northwest Research Station. 31 p.

Timber availability, aboveground tree biomass, and changes in aboveground carbon pools are important consequences of landscape management. There are several models available for calculating tree volume and aboveground tree biomass pools. This paper documents species-specific regional equations for tree volume and aboveground live tree biomass estimation that might be used to examine consequences of midscale landscape management in the Pacific Northwest. These regional equations were applied to a landscape in the upper Deschutes study area in central Oregon. We demonstrate an analysis of the changes in aboveground tree biomass and wood product availability at the scale of several watersheds on general forest lands under an active fuel-treatment management scenario. Our approach lays a foundation for further landscape management analysis, such as financial analysis of timber product and biomass supply, forest carbon sequestration, wildlife habitat suitability, and fuel reduction related studies.

Keywords: Timber products, biomass supply, volume equation, biomass equation, carbon storage, Pacific Northwest, central Oregon.

Contents

Introduction

Forest land managers and policymakers face substantial challenges in managing forest lands to meet evolving environmental, social, and economic demands. The Interagency Mapping and Assessment Project (IMAP) is an interagency[1] effort to develop midscale assessment and planning tools for addressing fire risks, fuel conditions, wildlife habitats, old forests, forest products, potential biomass supplies, and other landscape attributes. Interagency Mapping and Assessment Project integrates a suite of vegetation dynamics models with existing and potential vegetation information to project potential future vegetation conditions, natural disturbances, wildlife habitats, fuel conditions, and other landscape characteristics under different management approaches. The outputs from vegetation simulation models can be used for a variety of landscape analyses including timber products, biomass supply, and carbon accounting. In this report, we document the volume and biomass equations that can be used with IMAP models and illustrate the simulated changes over time in timber product availability and aboveground tree biomass in a central Oregon study area. The volume and biomass equations selected for use in the regional landscape study were the subject of comparison in an earlier paper (Zhou and Hemstrom 2009), in which the regional model was compared with other methods developed for broad-scale estimation.

Volume Equations for Landscape Analysis

Volume equations are expressions of tree forms used to estimate the cubic content of a tree with given three-dimensional shapes. Different tree species often have different shapes in the same region, or the same species may have different shapes in different regions. The Forest Inventory and Analysis (FIA) Program of the USDA Forest Service estimates total stem volume, merchantable volume, sawtimber volume, and other attributes from tree measurements on inventory plots. Three major types of timber volume estimation were summarized in the Timber Volume Estimator Handbook (USDA FS 1993). They are (1) stem profile equations, (2) direct volume estimators, and (3) product estimators. The Behre (1927) hyperbola, one of the stem profile models, has been used by the National Forest Systems in the Pacific Northwest Region (USDA FS 1978) for calculating tree volumes, whereas

---

[1] IMAP partners include USDA Forest Service Pacific Northwest Research Station, Pacific Northwest Region, Western Wildland Environmental Threats Center, Oregon Department of Forestry, Washington Department of Natural Resources, The Nature Conservancy, and others.

the FIA Program in the Pacific Northwest Research Station (PNW-FIA) is using the direct volume equation and the tarif system[2] for measured tree volume estimation.

For volume estimation in our midscale landscape study, we applied direct volume equations and the tarif system (Brackett 1973), the approach used by the PNW-FIA Program. Most of the equations were published from local tree studies and are documented by Waddell and Hiserote (2005). Two methods were used to calculate cubic volume in this approach: (1) using the cubic-foot volume of total stem from ground to tree tip (CVTS) to calculate the tarif number and the other volumes (table 1a); (2) using the cubic-foot volume from a 1-ft stump to a 4-in top (CV4) to calculate tarif number and other volumes (table 1b). These volume equations are for estimation of wood volume without bark. The defect is not included in the estimate.

Equations listed in table 1a allow direct estimation of CVTS for different Pacific Northwest tree species, and can be applied to all diameter classes if the equations for specified species are available. The tarif numbers are calculated based on CVTS (Brackett 1973). The other volumes such as cubic-foot volume from a 1-ft stump to the tree tip (CVT) and CV4 are derived from CVTS and tarif numbers.

Equations shown in table 1b calculate CV4 first, then the tarif numbers are derived from CV4 for calculating CVTS and CVT for trees over 5 inches in diameter at breast height (DBH). For trees less than 5 inches in DBH, the CVTS was calculated by using direct equations shown in the same table.

The saw-log volume estimates include saw-log cubic-foot volume (CV), Scribner volume (SV) and international volume (IV) (table 1c). The saw-log volume is the volume of wood in the central stem of a sample commercial species tree of sawtimber size (9.0 in DBH minimum for softwood and 11.0 in minimum for hardwood) from a 1-ft stump to a minimum diameter at top.

Volume equations do not exist for all tree species in the study area. For those species without a volume equation, we chose equations from species with similar growth forms. The volume estimations for this study may include:

1. Cubic-foot volume of the total stem from ground to tree tip (CVTS).
2. Cubic-foot volume from a 1-ft stump to the tree tip (CVT).
3. Cubic-foot volume from a 1-ft stump to a 4-in top (CV4).
4. Saw-log cubic-foot volume from a 1-ft stump to 6-in top for softwoods (CV6) and to an 8-in top for hardwoods (CV8).

---

[2] The tarif system is a comprehensive tree volume calculation procedure and was adapted from the European system to the Pacific Northwest. The tarif system provides a series of preconstructed local volume tables applicable to the specific stand. The volume computation procedure of the tarif system was presented in a flow chart by Brackett (1973).

5. Scribner board-foot volume to a 6-in top in 16-ft logs (SV616) and in 32-ft logs (SV632), and to an 8-in top in 16-ft logs (SV816) and in 32-ft logs (SV832).

6. International board-foot volume to a 6-in top (IV6) for softwood and to an 8-in top (IV8) for hardwood.

Biomass Equations for Midscale Landscape Analysis

Tree biomass estimation has become increasingly important for at least two reasons: (1) forest land plays an important role in carbon sequestration for mitigating global climate changes, and (2) biomass from forests might be used to generate energy. Various tree biomass calculation methods are applied on forest lands in the United States. The USDA Forest Service has used the Jenkins equation system (Jenkins et al. 2004) to assess forest biomass at national scales and for forest carbon estimates used in official greenhouse gas and carbon sequestration assessments for the United States (US EPA 2008). The national forest resources report for the Forest and Rangeland Renewable Resources Planning Act has used the component ratio method (CRM) to estimate tree biomass for consistency across regions. The objective of CRM is to provide national-scale biomass and carbon estimates consistent with FIA volume estimates at the tree level (Heath et al. 2008). However, these methods produce generalized biomass estimates compared to regional, detailed allometric equations (Zhou and Hemstrom 2009). Regional models are usually tree species-specific and result from detailed tree studies. We assume these regional models will be suitable for analyses of midscale landscapes (e.g., areas of hundreds of thousands to a few million acres).

Live tree biomass includes belowground biomass (root biomass) and aboveground biomass. We examined aboveground tree biomass using regional volume and biomass models including total stem wood biomass, bark biomass, and branch biomass. The foliage biomass is not included in this study.

Tree stem wood biomass from ground to tip (including stump) was estimated using volume equations (tables 1a, 1b, and 1c) multiplied by the wood density:

$$WB = (CVTS \times W_d)$$

where

CVTS = total stem volume from ground to tip (cubic feet) (tables 1a and 1b),

W_d = wood density (kilogram/cubic foot)[3],

WB = stem wood biomass (kilogram).

---

[3] Wood density is calculated by specific gravity times density of water (62.4 lb/ft^3 or 1000 kg/m^3).

The equations for estimating tree branch biomass are listed in table 2, and bark biomass equations are in table 3. These biomass equations are also from local tree studies, and most of them were from published papers and have been used for PNW-FIA live tree biomass estimation (Means et al. 1994, Waddell and Hiserote 2005). The assignments of volume, biomass equations for each major species within different geographic regions of the Pacific Northwest are in table 4. The specific gravities of wood and bark by species (Miles and Smith 2009) for calculating wood or bark density are presented in table 5.

There are important constraints to consider when applying these equations to measured tree data (tables 1a-c, 2, and 3). For example, bark biomass equations (27), (29), and (32) in table 3 may produce negative bark biomass when DBH is less than 2 in. We programmed those constraints along with the various volume and biomass equations into a SAS®[4] (SAS Institute Inc. 2008) script for our analysis.

Case Study

The upper Deschutes landscape is an area of about 2 million acres that extends from just north of Redmond, Oregon, to south of Gilchrist in central Oregon (fig. 1). We focused on the general forest lands managed by the USDA Forest Service for our analysis; about 500,000 ac, or 25 percent of the upper Deschutes landscape. General forest lands are outside reserved areas (e.g., late-successional reserves, wilderness, national monument). We modeled potential trends in forest vegetation structure and vegetation composition under the scenario of active fuel treatment management with natural disturbances (wildfire and insect outbreaks) that moved dry forests toward more open conditions dominated by large trees of early-seral species. This management scenario is likely much more active, in terms of area treated per year, than currently occurs on general forest lands. It is assumed in this scenario that general forest lands are managed for multiple uses, including restoration of forests to conditions more resistant to uncharacteristic wildfire and insect outbreaks, recreation, wildlife habitat, and generation of forest products (e.g., biomass and timber), and that some level of salvage may occur following stand-replacement natural disturbances, but that the level is generally low. The Vegetation Dynamics Development Tool (VDDT) (ESSA Technologies Ltd. 2007), a state-and-transition model, was used in this study. VDDT has been used in other similar landscape analyses in the interior Pacific Northwest (Hann et al. 1997, Hemstrom et al. 2007). We ran this active fuel-treatment scenario for 300 years with 30 Monte

---

[4] The use of trade or firm names in this publication is for reader information and does not imply endorsement by the U.S. Department of Agriculture of any product or service.

Carlo simulations of different combinations of fire and insect outbreaks using methods developed by Hemstrom et al. (2008).

Existing vegetation conditions came from Gradient Nearest Neighbor (GNN) imputation of inventory plots to 30-m pixels (Ohmann and Gregory 2002; http://www.fsl.orst.edu/lemma/method/methods.php). Each 30-m pixel with an associated inventory plot (PNW-FIA data and USDA Forest Service Pacific Northwest Region inventory data) was assigned to one of the state classes in the VDDT model. Then area is summarized in each state class within each watershed and ownership/allocation class to develop initial conditions for our models, breaking forest structure into classes that combine overstory tree size and canopy density:

1. Grass/forb, seedling, and sapling—Tree canopy less than 10 percent cover but potentially forested or trees less than 1 in DBH.
2. Pole—Tree canopy over 10 percent and dominant/co-dominant tree diameter 1 to 5 in DBH.

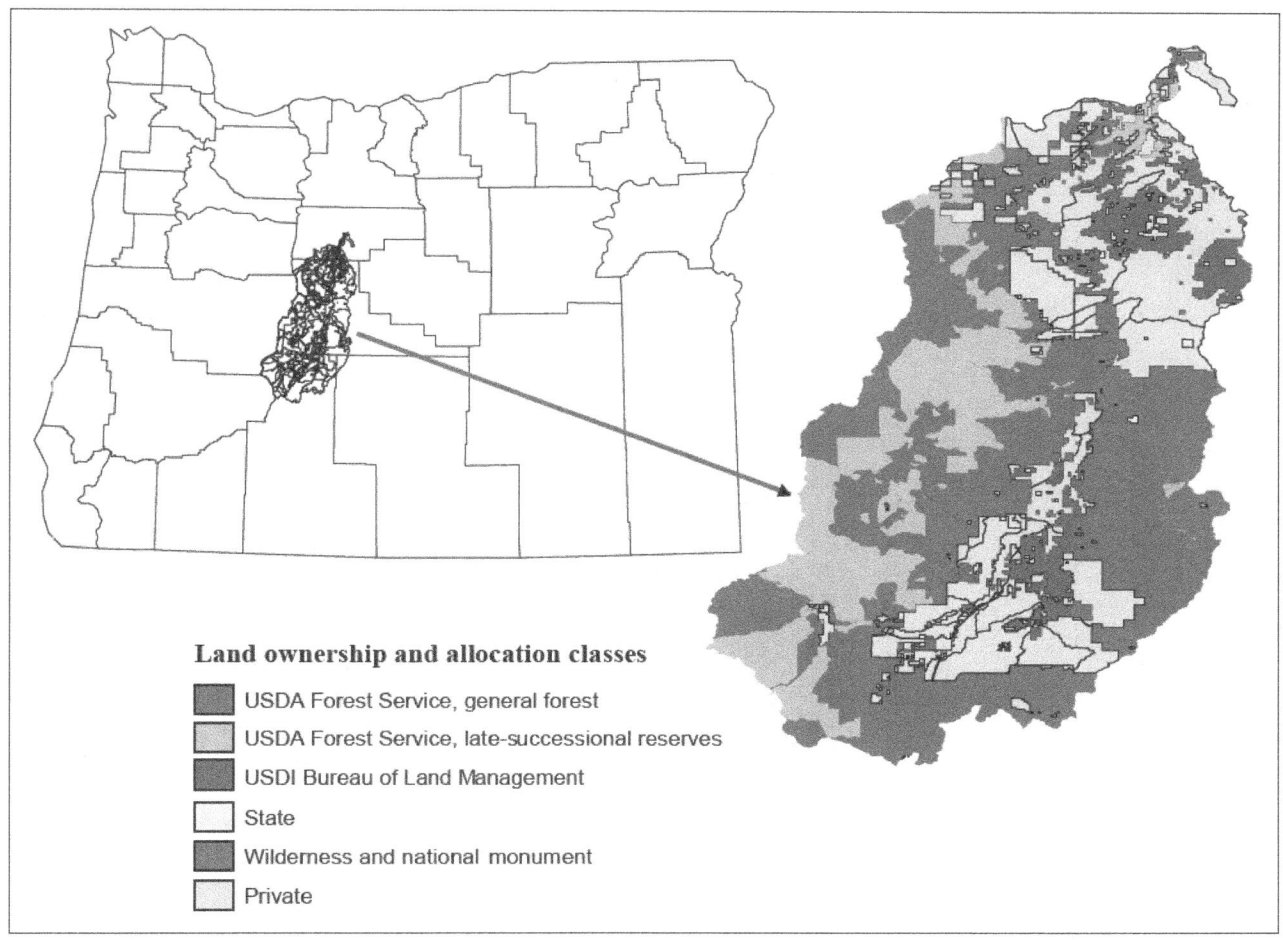

Land ownership and allocation classes

- USDA Forest Service, general forest
- USDA Forest Service, late-successional reserves
- USDI Bureau of Land Management
- State
- Wilderness and national monument
- Private

Figure 1—The upper Deschutes study area and land ownership/allocation classes in central Oregon.

3. Small tree—Tree canopy over 10 percent and dominant/co-dominant tree diameter 5 to 10 in DBH.

4. Medium tree—Tree canopy over 10 percent and dominant/co-dominant tree diameter 10 to 20 in DBH.

5. Large tree open—Tree canopy 40 to 60 percent cover and dominant/co-dominant tree diameter >20 in DBH.

6. Large tree closed—Tree canopy >60 percent cover and dominant/co-dominant tree diameter >20 in DBH.

The average volume and biomass are estimated using inventory plot data and allometric equations for each VDDT state class, with the same assignment of inventory plots to state classes. The result was a large look-up table that linked VDDT model state class to volume and biomass estimates. Landscape projections of changes to volume and biomass by watershed, ownership/allocation, and state class were developed by linking our volume and biomass look-up tables to modeled future area in each state class within landscape strata of watersheds and ownership/allocations. The process was coded and run in the SAS software package.

Results

Forests of seedlings/saplings, poles, small, and medium-sized trees currently dominate vegetation conditions in the study area (fig. 2). The active fuel-treatment scenario in this study produces a general forest landscape dominated by open stands of large trees with abundant openings over the 300-year simulation period.

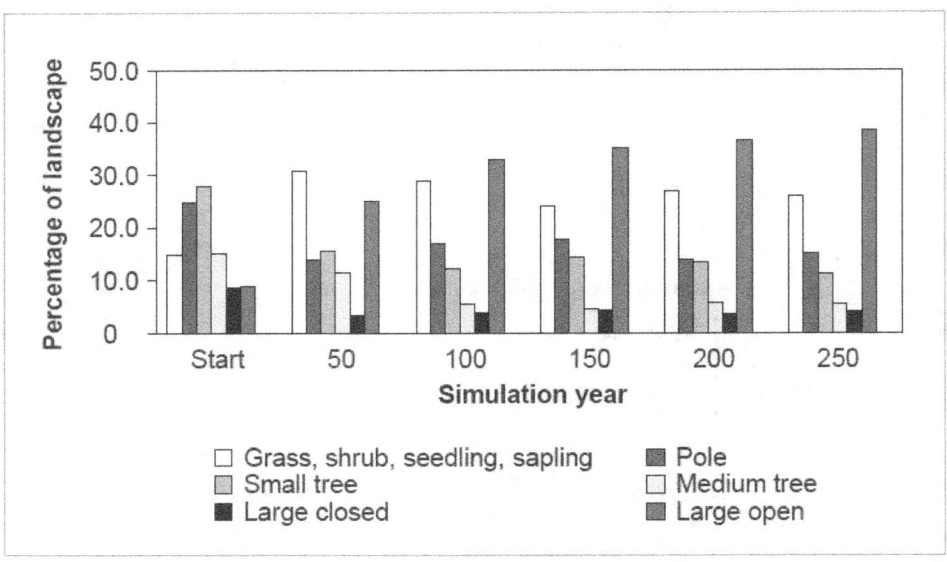

Figure 2—Proportion of the study area in forest structure classes over a 300-year simulation period in the study area.

At present, the standing pool of merchantable volume is 571 million cubic feet in the study area for general forest land, mostly in forest structure classes of small trees and relatively dense stands (figs. 2 and 3). Over the first 50 years of the 300-year simulation period, the standing pool of merchantable volume declined to 460 million cubic feet (fig. 3). Average 47 percent (range from 40 to 59 percent) of the total removal of live tree volume from the landscape in the first 50 years was from active treatments that generated forest products (including salvage) and the remaining from wildfires, insect outbreaks, and other disturbances where no salvage occurred. Initially, total loss of live tree volume was 170 million cubic feet per decade or 17 million cubic feet per year, but losses slowed and stabilized after 50 years. For the remaining 250 years of our simulations, the total removal was 50 million cubic feet per decade, or 5 million cubic feet per year. After 50 years, however, growth outpaced volume loss so that the landscape once again contained 570 million cubic feet of merchantable volume around simulation year 275. Much of the recovered volume is in the structure class of large trees of early-seral species (e.g., ponderosa pine) by the end of the simulation.

Pools of sawtimber follow a similar trajectory (fig. 4). The landscape sawtimber pool is currently 2.75 billion board feet, much of that in the structure classes of small (average 5 to 10 in DBH) and medium (average 10 to 20 in DBH) sized. Over the first 30 years, the sawtimber pool declines to 2.33 billion board feet. The sawtimber pool then begins to rebound and ends 17 percent above initial conditions

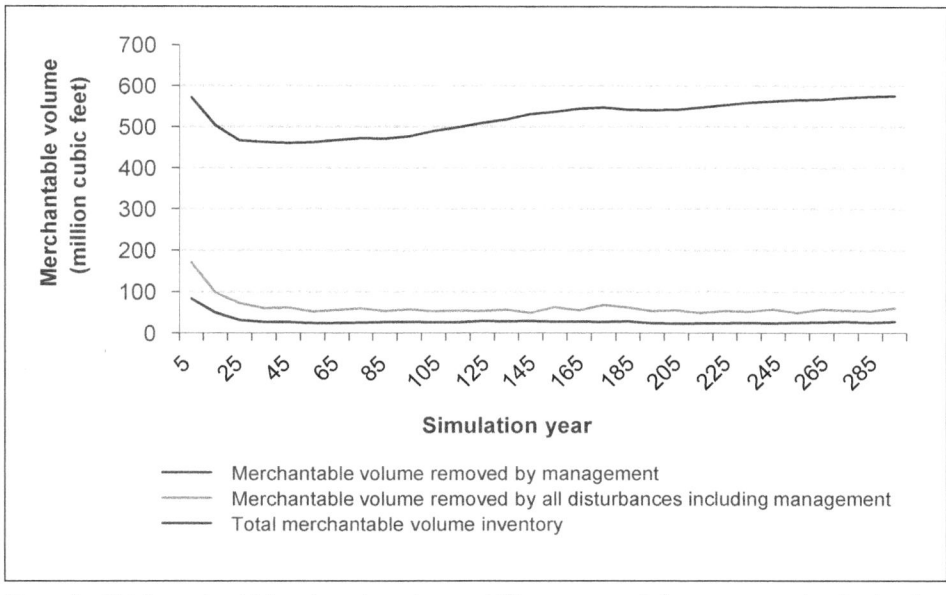

Figure 3—Total merchantable volume inventory and 10-year removals by management and natural disturbances.

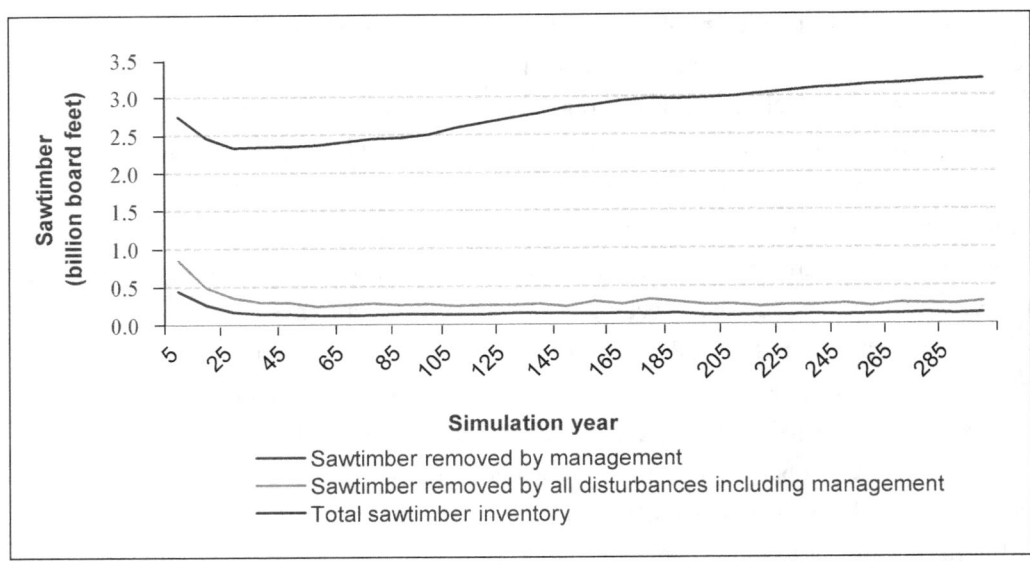

Figure 4—Total sawtimber volume inventory and 10-year removals by management and natural disturbances.

by the end of the 300-year simulation period. Timber harvest averages 50 percent (range from 43 to 62 percent) of the sawtimber removals during the 300-year projection period, and the remaining is from natural disturbances.

The pool of aboveground tree biomass in the study area begins at 12.6 million tons and declines to 10.2 million tons by the end of the first 50 years (fig. 5). Total annual removals of aboveground tree biomass decline from 0.4 million tons (or 4 million tons per decade) at the start of the simulation period to 0.15 million tons per

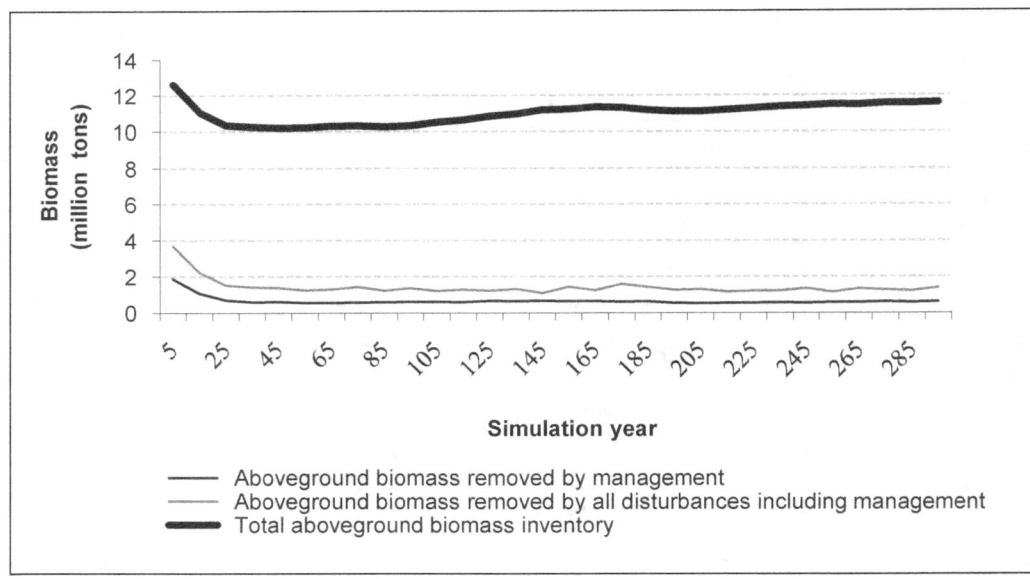

Figure 5—Total biomass inventory and 10-year removals by management and natural disturbances.

year (or 1.5 million tons per decade) after the third decade. Harvest averages 46 percent (range from 39 to 60 percent) of aboveground live tree biomass removals and the rest is from other natural disturbances. Over the last 250 years of the simulation period, the average annual removal is 1.2 percent of the total aboveground live tree biomass inventory. The total aboveground tree biomass pool does not quite recover to initial levels after 300 years, instead ending at 11.6 million tons.

Discussion

Active fuel treatment with natural disturbances interacted to produce substantial changes to landscape pools of aboveground live tree volume and biomass over 300 years in our simulations. The combination of timber harvest from fuel treatments and natural disturbances (wildfire and insect outbreaks) caused an initial decline of 14 to 19 percent in each pool over the first 30 to 50 simulation years. The pools then began slow recovery as growth on large, fire-resistant trees in open stands outstripped harvest and natural disturbance losses. Since our active fuel-treatment scenario was designed to reduce wildfire and insect outbreak losses rather than maximize timber output, the forested landscape pools continued to recover to levels equal to or above initial conditions over the last 250 years of the simulations. Interestingly, the sawtimber pool exceeded initial conditions by the end of the simulation because growth occurred on large trees that contain proportionately more sawtimber than the small and medium-sized trees that currently dominate the landscape.

The results in this study suggest that an active fuel-treatment management approach might initially reduce aboveground tree pools of volume, sawtimber, and live tree carbon stock but might, over the longer term, move forest conditions toward similar pool sizes in more sustainable forest conditions, as suggested by Boerner et al. (2008). It seems logical that open forests of large, fire-tolerant tree species would be less susceptible to sudden loss to severe wildfire or insect outbreaks (e.g., Hartsough et al. 2008, Hurteau and North 2009) though the effects of management on forest carbon pools are debatable (e.g., Finkral and Evans 2008, Harmon et al. 1996, Hudiburg et al. 2009, Hurteau and North 2009, Kurz et al. 1997). For example, Finkral and Evans (2008) estimated that thinning treatments in northern Arizona ponderosa pine stands released more carbon than stand-replacing wildfire might have, largely owing to the fate of thinned trees sold as firewood rather than for longer lasting wood products. They did not examine the longer term recovery of carbon on large, fire-tolerant trees. The fate of harvested trees was not examined in this active fuel-treatment scenario. It is suspected, however, that a similar result would apply; trees sold for firewood could quickly contribute to atmospheric carbon, whereas those destined to become long-term wood products would contribute more slowly.

Several cautions and needs are suggested for additional work. This study did not include the potential future effects of climate change in our active fuel-treatment scenario. Certainly, climate change could alter the rate of natural disturbances and tree growth, changing the aboveground pools. It also did not examine soil carbon changes that might accompany an active fuel-treatment management approach. It is possible that the active fuel-treatment scenario used in this study treats a much higher proportion of the general forest landscape than currently occurs and that modeling a current management scenario would produce considerably different results. However, a landscape modeling approach that includes dynamic interactions between management activities, natural disturbances, and tree growth over a long period is useful for considering management impacts on timber volume, aboveground tree biomass, and carbon storage.

Conclusions

Timber supply and biomass estimation can be important to landscape management analysis, depending on the questions asked. Although there are several models available for calculating tree volume and aboveground biomass, most of the species-specific regional volume and biomass equations presented in this paper are applied in the PNW-FIA Program (Donnegan et al. 2008), and these regional models would be suitable for mid- and fine-scale landscape analyses (Zhou and Hemstrom 2009). The application of these regional models to the upper Deschutes area provides an example of how such an analysis might be implemented at the scale of several or many watersheds. Localized information on trends in these landscape characteristics should help managers, policymakers, and others evaluate different management scenarios in terms of biomass, timber availability, and aboveground tree carbon pools over time. Because such analysis provides information at the scale of land ownerships within watersheds, the long-term conditions and sustainability of these pools could be mapped for midscale analysis and evaluation. This paper lays a foundation for further analyses of landscape management practices, such as financial analysis of timber products, biomass supply, and aboveground tree carbon sequestration for differing landscape management scenarios while including critical interactions with natural disturbances.

Equivalents

When you know:	Multiply by:	To get:
Acres (ac)	0.405	Hectares (ha)
Feet (ft)	.305	Meters (m)
Cubic feet (ft^3)	.0283	Cubic meters (m^3)
Inches (in)	2.54	Centimeters (cm)
Pounds (lb)	.454	Kilograms (kg)
Tons	.907	Metric tones
Pounds per cubic foot (lb/ft^3)	16.02	Kilograms per cubic meter (kg/m^3)

References

Behre, C.E. 1927. Form-class taper curve and volume tables and their application. Journal of Agricultural Research. 45(8): 673–744.

Bell, J.F.; Marshall, D.D.; Johnson, G.P. 1981. Tarif tables for mountain hemlock: developed from an equation of total stem cubic-foot volume. Res. Bull. 35. Corvallis, OR: Forest Research Laboratory, School of Forestry, Oregon State University. 45 p.

Boerner, R.E.J.; Huang, J.; Hart, S.C. 2008. Fire, thinning, and the carbon economy: effects of fire and fire surrogate treatments on estimated carbon storage and sequestration rate. Forest Ecology and Management. 255: 3081–3097.

Brackett, M. 1973. Notes on TARIF tree-volume computation. DNR Rep. 24. Olympia, WA: State of Washington, Department of Natural Resources. 26 p.

Chambers, C.; Foltz, B. 1979. The TARIF system--revisions and additions. DNR Note 27. Olympia, WA: State of Washington, Department of Natural Resources. 8 p.

Chittester, J.; MacLean, C. 1984. Cubic-foot tree-volume equations and tables for western juniper. Res. Note PNW-RN- 420. Portland, OR: U.S. Department of Agriculture, Forest Service, Pacific Northwest Forest and Range Experiment Station. 8 p.

Cochran, P.H.; Jennings, J.W.; Youngberg, C.T. 1984. Biomass estimators for thinned second-growth ponderosa pine trees. Res. Note PNW-RN-415. Portland, OR: U.S. Department of Agriculture, Forest Service, North Central Forest Experiment Station. 6 p.

Donnegan, J.; Campbell, S.; Azuma, D., tech. eds. 2008. Oregon's forest resources, 2001–2005: five-year Forest Inventory and Analysis report. Gen. Tech. Rep. PNW-GTR-765. Portland, OR: U.S. Department of Agriculture, Forest Service, Pacific Northwest Research Station. 186 p.

ESSA Technologies Ltd. 2007. Vegetation Dynamics Development tool user guide, Version 6.0. Vancouver, BC. 196 p.

Finkral, A.J.; Evans, A.M. 2008. The effect of a thinning treatment on carbon stock in a northern Arizona ponderosa pine forest. Forest Ecology and Management. 255: 2743–2750.

Gholz, H.L.; Campbell, A.G.; Brown, A.T. 1979. Equations for estimating biomass and leaf area of plants in the Pacific Northwest. Research Paper 41. Corvallis, OR: Forest Research Laboratory, Oregon State University. 39 p.

Halpern, C.; Means, J. 2004. Pacific Northwest plant biomass component equation library. Corvallis, OR: Long-Term Ecological Research, Forest Science Data Bank. http://andrewsforest.oregonstate.edu/data/abstract.cfm?dbcode=TP072. (September 24, 2009).

Hann, W.J.; Jones, J.L.; Karl, M.G.; Hessburg, P.F.; Keane, R.E.; Long, D.G.; Menakis, J.P.; McNicoll, C.H.; Leonard, S.G.; Gravenmier, R.A.; Smith, B.G. 1997. Landscape dynamics of the basin. In: Quigley, T.M.; Arbelbide, S.J., eds. An assessment of ecosystem components in the interior Columbia basin and portions of the Klamath and Great Basins. Gen. Tech. Rep. PNW-GTR-405. Portland, OR: U.S. Department of Agriculture, Forest Service, Pacific Northwest Research Station: 337–1055.

Harmon, M.E.; Garman, S.L.; Ferrell, W.K. 1996. Modeling historical patterns of tree utilization in the Pacific Northwest: carbon sequestration implications. Ecological Applications. 6: 641–652.

Hartsough, B.R.; Abrams, S.; Barbour, R.J.; Drews, E.S.; McIver, J.D.; Moghaddas, J.J.; Schwilk, D.W.; Stephens, S.L. 2008. The economics of alternative fuel reduction treatments in Western United States dry forests: financial and policy implications from the National Fire and Fire Surrogate Study. Forest Policy and Economics. 10: 344–354.

Heath, L.S.; Hansen, M.H.; Smith, J.E.; Smith, W.B.; Miles, P.D. 2008. Investigation into calculating tree biomass and carbon in the FIADB using a biomass expansion factor approach. In: McWilliams, W.; Moisen, G.; Czaplewski, R., comps. 2008 Forest Inventory and Analysis (FIA) symposium. Proc. RMRS-P-56 CD. Fort Collins, CO: U.S. Department of Agriculture, Forest Service, Rocky Mountain Research Station. [CD–ROM].

Hemstrom, M.A.; Merzenich, J.; Reger, A.; Wales, B. 2007. Integrated analysis of landscape management scenarios using state and transition models in the upper Grande Ronde River Subbasin, Oregon, USA. Landscape and Urban Planning. 80: 198–211.

Hemstrom, M.A.; Zhou, X.; Barbour, R.J.; Singleton, R.; Merzenich, J. 2008. Integrating natural disturbances and management activities to examine risks and opportunities in the central Oregon landscape analysis. In: Pye, J.M.; Rauscher, H.M.; Sands, Y.; Lee, D.C.; Beatty, J.S., eds. Encyclopedia of forest environmental threats, Portland, OR. http://www.threats.forestencyclopedia. net/p/p3389/p3390. (October 29, 2009).

Hudiburg, T.; Law, B.; Turner, D.P.; Campbell, J.; Donato, D.; Duane, M. 2009. Carbon dynamics of Oregon and northern California forests and potential land-based carbon storage. Ecological Applications. 19: 163–180.

Hurteau, M.; North, M. 2009. Fuel treatment effects on tree-based forest carbon storage and emissions under modeled wildfire scenarios. Frontiers in Ecology and the Environment. 7: 409–414.

Jenkins, J.C.; Chojnacky, D.C.; Heath, L.S.; Birdsey, R.A. 2004. A comprehensive database of biomass regressions for North American tree species. Gen. Tech. Rep. NE-319. Newtown Square, PA: U.S. Department of Agriculture, Forest Service, Northeastern Research Station. 45 p. [1 CD-ROM].

Krumland, B.E.; Wensel, L.E. 1975. Preliminary young growth volume tables for coastal California conifers. Res. Note 1. In-house memo. Berkeley, CA: Co-op Redwood Yield Research Project, Department of Forestry and Conservation, College of Natural Resources, University of California, Berkeley. On file with: Forest Inventory and Analysis Program, Pacific Northwest Research Station, 620 SW Main, Suite 400, Portland, OR 97205.

Kurz, W.A.; Beukema, S.J.; Apps, M.J. 1997. Carbon budget implications of the transition from natural to managed disturbance regimes in forest landscapes. Mitigation and Adaptation Strategies for Global Change. 2: 1381–2386.

MacLean, C.; Farrenkopf, T. 1983. Eucalyptus volume equation. In-house memo describing the volume equation for CVTS, to be used for all species of Eucalyptus. The equation was developed from 111 trees. On file with: Forest Inventory and Analysis Program, Pacific Northwest Research Station, 620 SW Main, Suite 400, Portland, OR 97205.

Means, J.E.; Hansen, H.A.; Koerper, G.J.; Alaback, P.B.; Klopsch, M.W. 1994. Software for computing plant biomass—BIOPAK users guide. Gen. Tech. Rep. PNW-GTR-340. Portland, OR: U.S. Department of Agriculture, Forest Service, Pacific Northwest Research Station. 184 p.

Miles, P.D.; Smith, W.B. 2009. Specific gravity and other properties of wood and bark for 156 tree species found in North America. Res. Note NRS-38. Newtown Square, PA: U.S. Department of Agriculture, Forest Service, Northern Research Station. 35 p.

Ohmann, J.; Gregory, M.J. 2002. Predictive mapping of forest composition and structure with direct gradient analysis and nearest neighbor imputation in coastal Oregon, U.S.A. Canadian Journal of Forestry. 32: 725–741.

Pillsbury, N.H.; Kirkley, M.L. 1984. Equations for total, wood, and saw-log volume for thirteen California hardwoods. Res. Note PNW-RN-414. Portland, OR: U.S. Department of Agriculture, Forest Service, Pacific Northwest Research Station. 52 p.

Sachs, D. 1983. Management effects on nitrogen nutrition and long-term productivity of western hemlock stands: an exercise in simulation with FORCYTE. Corvallis, OR: Oregon State University. 63 p. M.S. thesis.

SAS Institute Inc. 2008. SAS/STAT® 9.2 User's Guide. Cary, NC: SAS Institute Inc.

Shaw, D.L., Jr. 1977. Biomass equations for Douglas-fir, western hemlock, redcedar, and red alder in Washington and Oregon. Centralia, WA: Western Forestry Research Center, Weyerhaeuser Company. 18 p.

Standish, J.T.; Manning, G.H.; Demaerschalk, J.P. 1985. Development of biomass equations for British Columbia tree species. Info. Rep. BC-X-264. Victoria, BC: Canadian Forest Service, Pacific Forest Resource Center. 47 p.

Summerfield, E. 1980. In-house memo describing equations for Douglas-fir and ponderosa pine. State of Washington, Department of Natural Resources. On file with: Forest Inventory and Analysis Program, Pacific Northwest Research Station, 620 SW Main, Suite 400, Portland, OR 97205.

U.S. Department of Agriculture, Forest Service [USDA FS]. 1978. Diameter and volume procedures. Used by the R-6 timber cruise system. USFS–R6 sale preparation and valuation section. Portland, OR, Pacific Northwest Region. 13 p.

U.S. Department of Agriculture, Forest Service [USDA FS]. 1993. Timber volume estimator handbook. Forest Service Handb. FSH 2409.12a—Amend. 2409.12a-93-1. Washington, DC.

U.S. Environmental Protection Agency [US EPA]. 2008. Inventory of U.S. greenhouse gas emissions and sinks: 1990–2006. EPA 430-R-08-005. Washington, DC: Office of Atmospheric Program. 394 p. http://www.epa.gov/climatechange/emissions/downloads/08_CR.pdf. (September 2009).

Waddell, K.L.; Hiserote, B. 2005. The PNW-FIA integrated database and user guide and documentation. Version 2.0. [CD-ROM]. Portland, OR: U.S. Department of Agriculture, Forest Service, Pacific Northwest Research Station. http://www.fs.fed.us/pnw/fia/publications/data/data.shtml. (April 2009).

Zhou, X.; Hemstrom, M.A. 2009. Estimating aboveground tree biomass on forest land in the Pacific Northwest: a comparison of approaches. Res. Pap. PNW-RP-584. Portland, OR: U.S. Department of Agriculture, Forest Service, Pacific Northwest Research Station. 18 p.

Appendix

Table 1a—Pacific Northwest volume equations—group 1

Eqn	CVTS: Cubic-foot volume of total stem, ground to tip (DBH $\geq$ 1 inch or 2.5 cm)	Major species[a]	Reference
1	$CVTS = 10^{-3.21809 + 0.04948 \times \log(HT) \times \log(DBH) - 0.15664 \times (\log(DBH))^2 + 2.02132 \times \log(DBH)}$ $^{+ 1.63408 \times \log(HT) - 0.16185 \times (\log(HT))^2}$	Douglas-fir (PNWW)	Brackett 1973
2	$CVTS = e^{-6.110493 + 1.81306 \times \ln(DBH) + 1.083884 \times \ln(HT)}$	Douglas-fir (PNWE)	Summerfield 1980
3	$CVTS = e^{-6.5193 + 1.7131 \times \ln(DBH) + 1.2274 \times \ln(HT)}$	Douglas-fir (CA)	Krumland and Wensel 1975
4	$CVTS = 10^{-2.729937 + 1.909478 \times \log(DBH) + 1.085681 \times \log(HT)}$	Ponderosa pine (PNWE)	Brackett 1973
6	$CVTS = 10^{-2.72170 + 2.00857 \times \log(DBH) + 1.08620 \times \log(HT) - 0.00568 \times DBH}$	Western hemlock (WA/OR/CA)	Chambers and Foltz 1979
8	$CVTS = 10^{-2.464614 + 1.701993 \times \log(DBH) + 1.067038 \times \log(HT)}$	Western redcedar (PNWE/CA)	Brackett 1973
9	$CVTS = 10^{-2.379642 + 1.6823 \times \log(DBH) + 1.039712 \times \log(HT)}$	Western redcedar (PNWW)	Brackett 1973
10	$CVTS = 10^{-2.502332 + 1.864963 \times \log(DBH) + 1.004903 \times \log(HT)}$	True fir (PNWE)	Brackett 1973
11	$CVTS = 10^{-2.575642 + 1.806775 \times \log(DBH) + 1.094665 \times \log(HT)}$	True fir (PNWW)	Brackett 1973
12	$CVTS = 10^{-2.539944 + 1.841226 \times \log(DBH) + 1.034051 \times \log(HT)}$	Spruce (PNWE/CA)	Brackett 1973
13	$CVTS = 10^{-2.700574 + 1.754171 \times \log(DBH) + 1.164531 \times \log(HT)}$	Spruce (PNWW)	Brackett 1973
15	$CVTS = 10^{-2.615591 + 1.847504 \times \log(DBH) + 1.085772 \times \log(HT)}$	Lodgepole pine (WA/OR/CA)	Brackett 1973
17	$CVTS = 0.001106485 \times (DBH)^{1.8140497} \times (HT)^{1.2744923}$	Mountain hemlock (WA/OR/CA)	Bell et al. 1981
18	$CVTS = e^{-6.7013 + 1.7022 \times \ln(DBH) + 1.2979 \times \ln(HT)}$	Shasta red fir (WA/OR/CA)	Krumland and Wensel 1975
21	$CVTS = 0.005454154 \times DBH^2 \times \left[0.307089 + 0.000861576 \times HT - 0.00372552 \times DBH \times \dfrac{HT}{HT - 4.5}\right.$ $\left. \times HT \times \left(\dfrac{HT}{HT - 4.5}\right)^2\right]$	Western juniper (WA/OR/CA)	Chittester and MacLean 1984
22	$CVTS = 10^{-2.624325 + 1.847123 \times \log(DBH) + 1.044007 \times \log(HT)}$	Western larch (WA/OR)	Brackett 1973
24	$CVTS = e^{-6.2597 + 1.9967 \times \ln(DBH) + 0.9642 \times \ln(HT)}$	Redwood (CA/WOR)	Krumland and Wensel 1975

Table 1a—Pacific Northwest volume equations—group 1 (continued)

Eqn	CVTS: Cubic-foot volume of total stem, ground to tip (DBH ≥ 1 inch or 2.5 cm)	Major species[a]	Reference
25	$CVTS = 10^{-2.672775 + 1.920617 \times \log(DBH) + 1.074024 \times \log(HT)}$	Alder (WA)	Brackett 1973
27	$CVTS = 10^{-2.945047 + 1.803973 \times \log(DBH) + 1.238855 \times \log(HT)}$	Cottonwood (CA)	Brackett 1973
28	$CVTS = 10^{-2.635360 + 1.946034 \times \log(DBH) + 1.024793 \times \log(HT)}$	Aspen (CA)	Brackett 1973
29	$CVTS = 10^{-2.757813 + 1.911681 \times \log(DBH) + 1.105403 \times \log(HT)}$	Birch	Brackett 1973
30	$CVTS = 10^{-2.770324 + 1.885813 \times \log(DBH) + 1.119043 \times \log(HT)}$	Maple	Brackett 1973
31	$CVTS = 0.0016144 \times DBH^2 \times HT$	Eucalyptus (CA)	MacLean and Farrenkopf 1983

Other cubic foot volume calculated from CVTS (Brackett 1973):

1. CVT: cubic-foot volume above 1-ft stump (DBH ≥ 1 in):

$$CVT = CVTS \times \left(0.9679 - 0.1051 \times 0.5529^{(DBH - 1.5)}\right)$$

2. CV4: cubic-foot volume above 1-ft stump to 4-in top

If DBH < 5.0 inches: $CV4 = 0$

If DBH ≥ 5.0 inches: $CV4 = TARIF \times \dfrac{BA - 0.087266}{0.912733}$

$$TARIF = \frac{CVTS \times 0.912733}{1.033 \times \left(1.0 + 1.382937 \times e^{\left(-4.015292 \times \frac{DBH}{10}\right)}\right) \times \left(BA + 0.087266\right) - 0.174533}$$

Where:

Note: log in base 10, ln in natural base.
DBH = diameter at breast height (inches).
HT = total height (feet).
BA = basal area (square feet), BA = 0.005454154 × DBH².
Equation numbers may not be in consecutive order.
PNWW = Pacific Northwest West includes western Oregon and Washington.
PNWE = Pacific Northwest East includes eastern Oregon and Washington.
CA = California, OR = Oregon, WA = Washington, WOR = western Oregon.
[a] Major species—the species or similar species for which the equation was referred for use in reference.

Table 1b—Pacific Northwest volume equations—group 2 (Pillsbury and Kirkley 1984)

Eqn	CV4: Cubic-foot volume from a 1-foot stump to a 4-inch top (DBH ≥ 5.0)	CVTS: Cubic-foot volume of total stem, ground to tip (for DBH < 5.0 inch)	Major species[b]
32	$CV4 = 0.0055212937 \times DBH^{2.07202} \times HT^{0.77467}$	$CVTS = 0.0120372263 \times (0.155646 + 0.90182 \times DBH^{2.02232} \times HT^{0.68638})$	Giant chinkapin
33	$CV4 = 0.0016380753 \times DBH^{2.05910} \times HT^{1.05293}$	$CVTS = 0.0057821322 \times (-0.127917 + 0.96579 \times DBH^{1.94553} \times HT^{0.88389})$	California laurel
34	$CV4 = 0.0005774970 \times DBH^{2.19576} \times HT^{1.14078}$	$CVTS = 0.0058870024 \times (-1.719890 + 0.95354 \times DBH + 0.021968 \times HT^{1.94165} \times HT^{0.86562})$	Tanoak
35	$CV4 = 0.0009684363 \times DBH^{2.39565} \times HT^{0.98878}$	$CVTS = 0.0042870077 \times (-0.382890 + 0.93545 \times DBH^{2.33631} \times HT^{0.74872})$	California white oak
36	$CV4 = 0.0053866353 \times DBH^{2.61268} \times HT^{0.31103}$	$CVTS = 0.0191453191 \times (-0.785720 + 0.92472 \times DBH^{2.40248} \times HT^{0.28060})$	Englemann oak
37	$CV4 = 0.0034214162 \times DBH^{2.35347} \times HT^{0.69586}$	$CVTS = 0.0101786350 \times (0.083602 + 0.94782 \times DBH^{2.22462} \times HT^{0.57561})$	Bigleaf maple
38	$CV4 = 0.0036795695 \times DBH^{2.12635} \times HT^{0.83339}$	$CVTS = 0.0070538108 \times (-0.268240 + 0.95767 \times DBH^{1.97437} \times HT^{0.85034})$	California black oak
39	$CV4 = 0.0042324071 \times DBH^{2.53987} \times HT^{0.50591}$	$CVTS = 0.0125103008 \times (-0.173240 + 0.94403 \times DBH^{2.33089} \times HT^{0.46100})$	Blue oak
40	$CV4 = 0.0025616425 \times DBH^{1.99295} \times HT^{1.01532}$	$CVTS = 0.0067322665 \times (-0.013484 + 0.98155 \times DBH^{1.96628} \times HT^{0.83458})$	Pacific madrone
41	$CV4 = 0.0024277027 \times DBH^{2.25575} \times HT^{0.87108}$	$CVTS = 0.0072695058 \times (-0.307220 + 0.95956 \times DBH^{2.14321} \times HT^{0.74220})$	Oregon white oak
42	$CV4 = 0.0031670596 \times DBH^{2.32519} \times HT^{0.74348}$	$CVTS = 0.0097438611 \times (-0.191276 + 0.96147 \times DBH^{2.20527} \times HT^{0.61190})$	Canyon live oak
43	$CV4 = 0.0024574847 \times DBH^{2.53284} \times HT^{0.60764}$	$CVTS = 0.0065261029 \times (-0.757397 + 0.93475 \times DBH^{2.31958} \times HT^{0.62528})$	Coast live oak
44	$CV4 = 0.0041192264 \times DBH^{2.14915} \times HT^{0.77843}$	$CVTS = 0.0136818837 \times (0.048177 + 0.92953 \times DBH^{2.02989} \times HT^{0.63257})$	Interior live oak

Other cubic foot volume calculated from CVTS (Brackett 1973):

1. Volume of total stem (ground to tip) (CVTS):

If DBH < 5.0 inches: use CVTS equations for each species in this table.

If DBH ≥ 5.0 inches:

$$CVTS = TARIF \times \frac{(1.033 \times (1.0 + 1.382937 \times e^{(-4.015292 \times \frac{DBH}{10})}) \times (BA + 0.087266) - 0.174533)}{0.912733}$$

Where $TARIF = CV4 \times \dfrac{0.912733}{BA - 0.087266}$

2. Volume from 1-foot stump to the tip (CVT): $CVT = CVTS \times (0.9679 - 0.1051 \times 0.5529^{(DBH - 1.5)})$

DBH = diameter at breast height.

[a] Total volume in Pillsbury and Kirkley (1984) includes all stem and branch wood plus stump and bark but excludes roots and foliage. It is transformed to inside bark total volume based on the relationship between inside bark diameter and outside bark diameter in table 2 (Pillsbury and Kirkley 1984). It is applied only to trees with DBH < 5.0 inch. For trees above 5.0 inches in DBH, the CV4 and Tarif will be applied.

[b] Major species—the species or similar species for which the equation was referred for use in reference.

Equation numbers may not be in consecutive order.

Table 1c—Pacific Northwest volume equations—sawtimber volume calculation

Saw-log volume types	Saw-log volume equations
Saw-log cubic feet volume (cubic feet)	CV6: Softwood saw-log cubic-foot volume above 1-foot stump to a 6-inch top (DBH ≥ 9 in) $CV6 = CV4 \times (0.993 - 0.993 \times 0.62^{(DBH-6.0)})$
	CV8: Hardwood saw-log cubic foot volume above 1-foot stump to an 8-inch top (DBH ≥ 11 in) $CV8 = CV4 \times (0.983 - 0.983 \times 0.65^{(DBH-8.6)})$
Scribner volume (board feet)	Scribner volume to a 6-inch top
	1. In 16-foot log to 6-inch top (SV616) and to an 8-inch top (SV816): SV616 = CV6 × BCU1 $SV816 = SV616 \times (0.990 - 0.589 \times 0.484^{(DBH - 9.5)})$ Where BCU1 is the board-foot Scribner from cubic-foot ratio $$BCU1 = 10^{\left[0.174439 + 0.117594 \times \log(DBH) \times \log\left(\frac{TARIF}{0.912733}\right) - \frac{8.210585}{DBH^2} + 0.236693 \times \log\left(\frac{TARIF}{0.912733}\right) - 0.00001345 \times \left(\frac{TARIF}{0.912733}\right)^2 - 0.00001937 \times DBH^2\right]}$$
	2. In 32-foot log to 6-inch top (SV632) and to an 8-inch top (SV832): SV632 = SV6 × BF3216 $SV832 = SV632 \times (0.990 - 0.58 \times 0.484^{(DBH - 9.5)})$ Where $BF3216 = 1.001491 - \frac{6.924097}{TARIF} + 0.00001351 \times DBH^2$ (TARIF from table 1a and 1b)
International volume (board feet)	1. International volume to a 6-inch top (IV6): IV6 = CV6 × BCU2 Where $BCU2 = -2.902145 + 3.466328 \times \log(DBH \times TARIF) - 0.2765985 \times DBH - 0.00008205 \times TARIF^2 + \frac{11.29598}{DBH^2}$ (TARIF from table 1a and 1b)
	2. International volume to an 8-inch top (IV8): $IV8 = IV6 \times (0.990 - 0.55 \times 0.485^{(DBH - 9.5)})$

Note: Saw-log volume is the volume of wood in the central stem of a sample commercial species tree of sawtimber size (9.0 inches DBH minimum for softwood and 11.0 inches minimum for hardwood) from a 1-foot stump to a minimum diameter at top.
Sources: Brackett 1973, Chambers and Foltz 1979.

Table 2—Pacific Northwest tree branch biomass (BCH) equations

Eqn	Branch equation	Major species[a]	Reference
1	$BCH = 13.0 + 12.4 \times \left(\dfrac{DBH\_cm}{100}\right)^2 \times H\_m$	Grand fir	Standish et al. 1985
2	$BCH = 3\,6 + 44\,2 \times \left(\dfrac{DBH\_cm}{100}\right)^2 \times H\_m$	Subalpine fir	Standish et al. 1985
3	$BCH = e^{-4\,1817 + 2\,3324 \times \ln(DBH\_cm)}$	Noble fir	Gholz et al. 1979
4	$BCH = 16.8 + 14.4 \times \left(\dfrac{DBH\_cm}{100}\right)^2 \times H\_m$	Engelmann spruce	Standish et al. 1985
5	$BCH = 9.7 + 22.0 \times \left(\dfrac{DBH\_cm}{100}\right)^2 \times H\_m$	Sitka spruce	Standish et al. 1985
6	$BCH = e^{-3.6941 + 2.1382 \times \ln(DBH\_cm)}$	Douglas-fir (PNWW)	Gholz et al. 1979
7	$BCH = e^{-4\,1068 + 1\,5177 \times \ln(DBH\_cm) + 1\,0424 \times \ln(H\_m)}$	Ponderosa pine	Cochran et al. 1984
8	$BCH = e^{-7\,637 + 3\,3648 \times \ln(DBH\_cm)}$	Sugar pine	Gholz et al. 1979
9	$BCH = 9.5 + 16.8 \times \left(\dfrac{DBH\_cm}{100}\right)^2 \times H\_m$	Western white pine	Standish et al. 1985
10	$BCH = 0.199 + 0.00381 \times (DBH\_cm)^2 \times H\_m$	Western redcedar	Shaw 1977
11	$BCH = 7.8 + 12.3 \times \left(\dfrac{DBH\_cm}{100}\right)^2 \times H\_m$	Lodgepole pine	Standish et al. 1985
12	$BCH = e^{-4.570 + 2.271 \times \ln(DBH\_cm)}$	Western hemlock	Sachs 1983
13	$BCH = e^{-7.2775 + 2.3337 \times \ln(DBH\_cm)}$	Western juniper	Gholz et al. 1979
14	$BCH = 1.7 + 26.2 \times \left(\dfrac{DBH\_cm}{100}\right)^2 \times H\_m$	Quaking aspen	Standish et al. 1985
15	$BCH = 2.5 + 36.8 \times \left(\dfrac{DBH\_cm}{100}\right)^2 \times H\_m$	Black cottonwood	Standish et al. 1985
16	$BCH = 8.1 + 21.5 \times \left(\dfrac{DBH\_cm}{100}\right)^2 \times H\_m$	Red alder	Standish et al. 1985
17	$BCH = e^{-5.2581 + 2.6045 \times \ln(DBH\_cm)}$	Mountain hemlock (CA)	Gholz et al. 1979
18	$BCH = 4.5 + 22.7 \times \left(\dfrac{DBH\_cm}{100}\right)^2 \times H\_m$	Pacific silver fir	Standish et al. 1985
19	$BCH = 5.3 + 9.7 \times \left(\dfrac{DBH\_cm}{100}\right)^2 \times H\_m$	Alaska yellow-cedar	Standish et al. 1985

Table 2—Pacific Northwest tree branch biomass (BCH) equations (continued)

Eqn	Branch equation	Major species[a]	Reference
20	$BCH = 20.4 + 7.7 \times \left(\dfrac{DBH\_cm}{100}\right)^2 \times H\_m$	Western larch	Standish et al. 1985
22	$BCH = 12.6 + 23.5 \times \left(\dfrac{DBH\_cm}{100}\right)^2 \times H\_m$	Douglas-fir	Standish et al. 1985
23	$BCH = 0.047 + 0.00413 \times (DBH\_cm)^2 \times H\_m$	Western hemlock (OR/WA)	Shaw 1977
24	$BCH = 4.2 + 17.4 \times \left(\dfrac{DBH\_cm}{100}\right)^2 \times H\_m$	Mountain hemlock (OR/WA)	Standish et al. 1985
25	$BCH = -0.6 + 45.1 \times \left(\dfrac{DBH\_cm}{100}\right)^2 \times H\_m$	White birch (OR/WA)	Standish et al. 1985

Note:

1. Biomass in kilogram (kg), DBH_cm is diameter in centimeters (cm), H_m is tree height in meters (m).
2. For branch equation 12, if site is thinned, the coefficient -4.570 will be replaced with -4.876 and all the other items kept the same.
3. Branch equation 25 may produce negative numbers when DBH < 3.5 inches, so it is suggested to use constraint: branch biomass = 0 when formulas produce negative numbers.
4. PNWW = Pacific Northwest West includes western Oregon and Washington.
5. CA = California, OR = Oregon, WA = Washington, WOR = western Oregon.

[a] Major species—the species or similar species for which the equation was referred for use in reference.

Table 3—Pacific Northwest tree bark biomass (BRK) equations

Eqn	Bark equation	Major species[a]	Reference
1	$BRK = \dfrac{1}{1000}\, e^{\,2.1069 + 2.7271 \times \ln(DBH\_cm)}$	White fir	Halpern and Means 2004
2	$BRK = 0.6 + 16.4 \times \left(\dfrac{DBH\_cm}{100}\right)^2 \times H\_m$	Grand fir	Standish et al. 1985
3	$BRK = 1.0 + 17.2 \times \left(\dfrac{DBH\_cm}{100}\right)^2 \times H\_m$	Subalpine fir	Standish et al. 1985
4	$BRK = \dfrac{1}{1000}\, e^{\,1.47146 + 2.8421 \times \ln(DBH\_cm)}$	California (Shasta) red fir	Halpern and Means 2004
5	$BRK = \dfrac{1}{1000}\, e^{\,2.79189 + 2.4313 \times \ln(DBH\_cm)}$	Noble fir	Halpern and Means 2004
6	$BRK = 1.3 + 12.6 \times \left(\dfrac{DBH\_cm}{100}\right)^2 \times H\_m$	Sitka spruce	Standish et al. 1985
7	$BRK = 4.5 + 9.3 \times \left(\dfrac{DBH\_cm}{100}\right)^2 \times H\_m$	Engelmann spruce	Standish et al. 1985
8	$BRK = 3.1 + 15.6 \times \left(\dfrac{DBH\_cm}{100}\right)^2 \times H\_m$	Douglas-fir (PNWW/CA)	Standish et al. 1985
9	$BRK = e^{\,-3.6263 + 1.34077 \times \ln(DBH\_cm) + 0.8567 \times \ln(H\_m)}$	Ponderosa pine	Cochran et al. 1984
10	$BRK = \dfrac{1}{1000}\, e^{\,2.183174 + 2.6610 \times \ln(DBH\_cm)}$	Sugar pine	Halpern and Means 2004
11	$BRK = 1.2 + 11.2 \times \left(\dfrac{DBH\_cm}{100}\right)^2 \times H\_m$	Western white pine	Standish et al. 1985
12	$BRK = \dfrac{1}{1000}\, e^{\,0.500948 + 2.8594 \times \ln(DBH\_cm)}$	Incense-cedar	Halpern and Means 2004
13	$BRK = 0.336 + 0.00058 \times (DBH\_cm)^2 \times H\_m$	Western redcedar	Shaw 1977
14	$BRK = 3.2 + 9.1 \times \left(\dfrac{DBH\_cm}{100}\right)^2 \times H\_m$	Lodgepole pine	Standish et al. 1985
15	$BRK = e^{\,-4.371 + 2.259 \times \ln(DBH\_cm)}$	Western hemlock	Sachs 1983
16	$BRK = e^{\,-10.175 + 2.63333 \times \ln(DBH\_cm \times 3.141593)}$	Western juniper	Gholz et al. 1979

Table 3—Pacific Northwest tree bark biomass (BRK) equations (continued)

Eqn	Bark equation	Major species[a]	Reference
17	$BRK = \dfrac{1}{1000}\, e^{7.189689 + 1.5837 \times \ln(DBH\_cm)}$	Giant sequoia	Halpern and Means 2004
18	$BRK = 1.3 + 27.6 \times \left(\dfrac{DBH\_cm}{100}\right)^2 \times H\_m$	Quaking aspen	Standish et al. 1985
20	$BRK = 1.2 + 24.0 \times \left(\dfrac{DBH\_cm}{100}\right)^2 \times H\_m$	Red alder	Standish et al. 1985
21	$BRK = 0.9 + 27.4 \times \left(\dfrac{DBH\_cm}{100}\right)^2 \times H\_m$	Mountain hemlock	Standish et al. 1985
22	$BRK = 1.0 + 15.6 \times \left(\dfrac{DBH\_cm}{100}\right)^2 \times H\_m$	Pacific silver fir	Standish et al. 1985
23	$BRK = 1.8 + 9.6 \times \left(\dfrac{DBH\_cm}{100}\right)^2 \times H\_m$	Alaska yellow-cedar	Standish et al. 1985
24	$BRK = 2.4 + 15.0 \times \left(\dfrac{DBH\_cm}{100}\right)^2 \times H\_m$	Western larch	Standish et al. 1985
25	$BRK = 3.6 + 18.2 \times \left(\dfrac{DBH\_cm}{100}\right)^2 \times H\_m$	Douglas-fir (PNWE)	Standish et al. 1985
26	$BRK = 0.025 + 0.00134 \times (DBH\_cm)^2 \times H\_m$	Western hemlock (OR/WA)	Shaw 1977
27	$BRK = 1.2 + 29.1 \times \left(\dfrac{DBH\_cm}{100}\right)^2 \times H\_m$	Paper birch	Standish et al. 1985
28	$BRK = 1.2 + 15.5 \times \left(\dfrac{DBH\_cm}{100}\right)^2 \times H\_m$	Black cottonwood	Standish et al. 1985
29	$BRK = 0.0000246916 \times H\_m^{0.69589} \times \left[\left(\dfrac{DBH\_cm - 0.21235}{0.94782}\right)^{2.35347} - DBH\_cm^{2.35347}\right] \times 35.30 \times B_d$	Pacific dogwood	Pillsbury and Kirkley 1984
30	$BRK = 0.0000386403 \times H\_m^{0.83339} \times \left[\left(\dfrac{DBH\_cm + 0.68133}{0.95767}\right)^{2.12635} - DBH\_cm^{2.12635}\right] \times 35.30 \times B_d$	California black oak	Pillsbury and Kirkley 1984
31	$BRK = 0.0000248325 \times H\_m^{0.74348} \times \left[\left(\dfrac{DBH\_cm + 0.48584}{0.96147}\right)^{2.32519} - DBH\_cm^{2.32519}\right] \times 35.30 \times B_d$	Canyon live oak	Pillsbury and Kirkley 1984

Table 3—Pacific Northwest tree bark biomass (BRK) equations (continued)

Eqn	Bark equation	Major species[a]	Reference
32	$BRK = 0.0000568840 \times H\_m^{0.77467} \times \left(\left(\dfrac{DBH\_cm + 0.39534}{0.90182} \right)^{2.07202} - DBH\_cm^{2.07202} \right) \times 35.30 \times B_d$	Golden chinkapin	Pillsbury and Kirkley 1984
33	$BRK = 0.0000237733 \times H\_m^{1.05293} \times \left(\left(\dfrac{DBH\_cm + 0.32491}{0.96579} \right)^{2.05910} - DBH\_cm^{2.05910} \right) \times 35.30 \times B_d$	California laurel	Pillsbury and Kirkley 1984
34	$BRK = 0.0000378129 \times H\_m^{1.01532} \times \left(\left(\dfrac{DBH\_cm + 0.03425}{0.98155} \right)^{1.99295} - DBH\_cm^{1.99295} \right) \times 35.30 \times B_d$	Pacific mandrone	Pillsbury and Kirkley 1984
35	$BRK = 0.0000236325 \times H\_m^{0.87108} \times \left(\left(\dfrac{DBH\_cm + 0.78034}{0.95956} \right)^{2.25575} - DBH\_cm^{2.25575} \right) \times 35.30 \times B_d$	Oregon white oak	Pillsbury and Kirkley 1984
36	$BRK = 0.0000081905 \times H\_m^{1.14078} \times \left(\left(\dfrac{DBH\_cm + 4.1177141}{0.95354} \right)^{2.19576} - DBH\_cm^{2.19576} \right) \times 35.30 \times B_d$	Tanoak	Pillsbury and Kirkley 1984

Equations 29 to 36 are transformed based on Pillsbury and Kirkley (1984);
log in base 10, ln in natural base.
Note:
(1) Biomass in kilograms (kg), DBH_cm is diameter in centimeters (cm), H_m is tree height in meters (m).
(2) B_d is bark density in kilograms per cubic foot (kg/ft³).
(3) Bark equations 27, 29, and 32 may produce negative bark biomass when DBH < 2 inches, so it is suggested to use constraint: bark biomass = 0 when formulas produce negative numbers.
(4) PNWW = Pacific Northwest West includes western Oregon and Washington.
PNWE = Pacific Northwest East includes eastern Oregon and Washington.
CA = California, OR = Oregon, WA = Washington, WOR = western Oregon.
[a] Major species—the species or similar species for which the equation was referred for use in reference.

Table 4—Assignment of volume and biomass equations to major tree species in the study region

Species code	Common name	Volume equation[a]			Branch equation[b]			Bark equation[c]		
		PNWW	PNWE	CA	PNWW	PNWE	CA	PNWW	PNWE	CA
11	Pacific silver fir	11	10	11	18	18	18	22	22	22
14	Santa Lucia fir or bristlecone fir	18	18	18	1	1	1	2	2	2
15	White fir	18	18	18	1	1	1	1	1	1
17	Grand fir	11	10	18	1	1	1	2	2	2
19	Subalpine fir	11	10	18	2	2	2	3	3	3
20	California red fir	18	18	18	3	3	3	4	4	4
21	Shasta red fir	18	18	18	3	3	3	4	4	4
22	Noble fir	11	10	18	3	3	3	5	5	5
41	Port-Orford-cedar	9	9	8	10	10	10	13	13	13
42	Alaska yellow-cedar	9	8	8	19	19	10	23	23	13
50	Cypress	9	9	9	10	10	10	13	13	13
51	Arizona cypress	9	9	9	10	10	10	13	13	13
54	Monterey cypress	9	9	9	10	10	10	13	13	13
55	Sargent's cypress	9	9	9	10	10	10	13	13	13
56	McNab cypress	9	9	9	10	10	10	13	13	13
62	California juniper	21	21	21	13	13	13	16	16	16
64	Western juniper	21	21	21	13	13	13	16	16	16
65	Utah juniper	21	21	21	13	13	13	16	16	16
66	Rocky Mountain juniper	21	21	21	13	13	13	16	16	16
72	Subablpine larch	22	22	22	20	20	20	24	24	24
73	Western larch	22	22	22	20	20	20	24	24	24
81	Incense-cedar	9	9	9	10	10	10	13	13	13
92	Brewer spruce	13	12	12	4	4	4	7	7	7
93	Engelmann spruce	13	12	12	4	4	4	7	7	7
98	Sitka spruce	13	12	12	5	5	5	6	6	6
101	Whitebark pine	15	15	15	9	9	9	11	11	11
102	Bristlecone pine	15	15	15	11	11	11	14	14	14
103	Knobcone pine	15	15	15	11	11	11	14	14	14
104	Foxtail pine	15	15	15	11	11	11	14	14	14
108	Lodgepole pine	15	15	15	11	11	11	14	14	14
109	Coulter pine	4	4	4	7	7	7	9	9	9
113	Limber pine	15	15	15	11	11	11	14	14	14
116	Jeffrey pine	4	4	4	11	11	11	9	9	9
117	Sugar pine	4	4	4	8	8	8	10	10	10
119	Western white pine	15	15	4	9	9	9	11	11	11
120	Bishop pine	15	15	15	11	11	11	14	14	14
122	Ponderosa pine	4	4	4	7	7	7	9	9	9
124	Monterey pine	15	15	15	11	11	11	14	14	14
127	Gray pine	4	4	4	7	7	7	9	9	9
130	Scotch pine	17	17	17	24	24	17	21	21	21
133	Singleleaf pinyon	21	21	21	13	13	13	16	16	16
137	Washoe pine	4	4	4	7	7	7	9	9	9
201	Bigcone Douglas-fir	1	2	3	6	22	6	8	25	8
202	Douglas-fir	1	2	3	6	22	6	8	25	8
211	Redwood	24	24	24	10	10	10	17	17	17
212	Giant sequoia	24	24	24	10	10	10	17	17	17
231	Pacific yew	9	8	8	10	10	10	13	13	13
242	Western redcedar	9	8	8	10	10	10	13	13	13

Table 4—Assignment of volume and biomass equations to major tree species in the study region (continued)

Species code	Common name	Volume equation[a]			Branch equation[b]			Bark equation[c]		
		PNWW	PNWE	CA	PNWW	PNWE	CA	PNWW	PNWE	CA
251	California nutmeg	9	8	8	10	10	10	13	13	13
263	Western hemlock	6	6	6	23	23	12	26	26	15
264	Mountain hemlock	17	17	17	24	24	17	21	21	21
298	Unknown softwood	17	17	17	24	24	17	21	21	21
312	Bigleaf maple	37	37	37	16	16	16	20	20	20
313	Boxelder	38	38	38	16	16	16	30	30	30
321	Rocky Mountain maple	30	30	30	16	16	16	20	20	20
322	Bigtooth maple	30	30	30	16	16	16	20	20	20
326	Chinkapin oak	43	43	43	16	16	16	31	31	31
330	Buckeye	43	43	43	16	16	16	31	31	31
333	California buckeye	43	43	43	16	16	16	31	31	31
341	Tree of heaven	28	28	28	14	14	14	18	18	18
351	Red alder	25	25	25	16	16	16	20	20	20
352	White alder	25	25	25	16	16	16	20	20	20
361	Pacific madrone	40	40	40	16	16	16	34	34	34
374	Water birch	25	25	25	25	25	25	27	27	27
375	Paper birch	25	25	25	25	25	25	27	27	27
376	Western paper birch	25	25	25	25	25	25	27	27	27
431	Golden chinkapin	32	32	32	16	16	16	32	32	32
475	Curlleaf mountain-mahogany	32	32	32	16	16	16	32	32	32
492	Pacific dogwood	25	25	25	16	16	16	29	29	29
500	Hawthorn	34	34	34	15	15	15	36	36	36
510	Eucalyptus	31	31	31	15	15	15	36	36	36
511	Tasmanian bluegum	31	31	31	15	15	15	36	36	36
540	Ash	38	38	38	16	16	16	20	20	20
542	Oregon ash	38	38	38	16	16	16	20	20	20
591	Holly	29	29	29	25	25	25	27	27	27
600	Walnut	38	38	38	16	16	16	30	30	30
603	Northern California walnut	38	38	38	16	16	16	30	30	30
631	Tanoak	34	34	34	15	15	15	36	36	36
660	Apple	42	42	42	15	15	15	31	31	31
730	California sycamore	27	27	27	15	15	15	28	28	28
740	Cottonwood and poplar spp.	27	27	27	15	15	15	28	28	28
741	Balsam poplar	27	27	27	15	15	15	28	28	28
742	Eastern cottonwood	27	27	27	15	15	15	28	28	28
745	Plains cottonwood	27	27	27	15	15	15	28	28	28
746	Quaking aspen	28	28	28	14	14	14	18	18	18
747	Black cottonwood	27	27	27	15	15	15	28	28	28
748	Fremont cottonwood	27	27	27	15	15	15	28	28	28
755	Mesquite	27	27	27	15	15	15	28	28	28
756	Western honey mesquite	27	27	27	15	15	15	28	28	28
758	Screwbean mesquite	27	27	27	15	15	15	28	28	28
760	Cherry	27	27	27	15	15	15	28	28	28
763	Chokecherry	27	27	27	15	15	15	28	28	28
768	Bitter cherry	27	27	27	15	15	15	28	28	28
800	Oak-deciduous	43	43	43	15	15	15	31	31	31
801	California live oak	43	43	43	15	15	15	31	31	31
805	Canyon live oak	42	42	42	15	15	15	31	31	31
807	Blue oak	39	39	39	15	15	15	30	30	30

Table 4—Assignment of volume and biomass equations to major tree species in the study region (continued)

Species code	Common name	Volume equation[a]			Branch equation[b]			Bark equation[c]		
		PNWW	PNWE	CA	PNWW	PNWE	CA	PNWW	PNWE	CA
810	Emory oak	39	39	39	15	15	15	30	30	30
811	Englemann oak	36	36	36	15	15	15	30	30	30
815	Oregon white oak	41	41	41	15	15	15	35	35	35
818	California black oak	38	38	38	15	15	15	30	30	30
821	California white oak	35	35	35	15	15	15	35	35	35
839	Interior live oak	44	44	44	15	15	15	31	31	31
901	Black locust	41	41	41	15	15	15	35	35	35
920	Willow	40	40	40	15	15	15	34	34	34
922	Black willow	40	40	40	15	15	15	34	34	34
926	Balsam willow	40	40	40	15	15	15	34	34	34
928	Scouler's willow	40	40	40	15	15	15	34	34	34
981	California-laurel	33	33	33	14	14	14	33	33	33
990	Tesota (desert ironwood)	33	33	33	14	14	14	33	33	33
998	Unknown hardwood	25	25	41	16	16	16	20	20	20
999	Unknown tree	25	25	25	16	16	16	20	20	20

Note: Tree species code (SPP) 298 and 326 in the table are not in the Forest Inventory and Analysis tree species list, but are defined in the study area.

PNWW = Pacific Northwest West includes western Oregon and Washington.

PNWE = Pacific Northwest East includes eastern Oregon and Washington.

CA = California,

[a] Equation numbers refer to those in table 1a and 1b.

[b] Equation numbers refer to numbers in table 2.

[c] Equation numbers refer to numbers in table 3.

Table 5—Specific gravity for major tree species wood and bark

FIA code	Common name	Scientific name	Wood-specific gravity	Bark-specific gravity
11	Pacific silver fir	*Abies amabilis* (Douglas ex Louden) Douglas ex Forbes	0.4	0.44
14	Santa Lucia or bristlecone fir	*Abies bracteata* (D. Don) D. Don ex Poit.	0.36	0.49
15	White fir	*Abies concolor* (Gord. & Glend.) Lindl. ex Hildebr.	0.37	0.56
17	Grand fir	*Abies grandis* (Douglas ex D. Don) Lindl.	0.35	0.57
19	Subalpine fir	*Abies lasiocarpa* (Hook.) Nutt.	0.31	0.5
20	California red fir	*Abies magnifica* A. Murray	0.36	0.44
21	Shasta red fir	*Abies x shastensis* (Lemmon) Lemmon [*magnifica × procera*]	0.36	0.49
22	Noble fir	*Abies procera* Rehd.	0.37	0.49
41	Port-Orford-cedar	*Chamaecyparis lawsoniana* (A. Murr.) Parl.	0.39	0.4
42	Alaska yellow-cedar	*Chamaecyparis nootkatensis* (D. Don) Spach	0.42	0.4
50	Cypress	*Cupressus* L.	0.41	0.42
51	Arizona cypress	*Cupressus arizonica* Greene ssp. *arizonica*	0.41	0.42
54	Monterey cypress	*Cupressus macrocarpa* Hartw. ex Gord.	0.41	0.42
55	Sargent's cypress	*Cupressus sargentii* Jeps.	0.41	0.42
56	MacNab's cypress	*Cupressus macnabiana* A. Murray	0.41	0.42
62	California juniper	*Juniperus californica* Carrière	0.45	0.4
64	Western juniper	*Juniperus occidentalis* Hook.	0.45	0.4
65	Utah juniper	*Juniperus osteosperma* (Torr.) Little	0.68	0.4
66	Rocky Mountain juniper	*Juniperus scopulorum* Sarg.	0.45	0.4
72	Subalpine larch	*Larix lyallii* Parl.	0.49	0.32
73	Western larch	*Larix occidentalis* Nutt.	0.48	0.33
81	Incense-cedar	*Calocedrus decurrens* (Torr.) Florin	0.35	0.25
92	Brewer spruce	*Picea breweriana* S. Watson	0.36	0.44
93	Engelmann spruce	*Picea engelmannii* Parry ex Engelm.	0.33	0.51
98	Sitka spruce	*Picea sitchensis* (Bong.) Carr.	0.33	0.55
101	Whitebark pine	*Pinus albicaulis* Engelm.	0.43	0.4
102	Rocky Mountain bristlecone pine	*Pinus aristata* Engelm.	0.43	0.4
103	Knobcone pine	*Pinus attenuata* Lemmon	0.39	0.38
104	Foxtail pine	*Pinus balfouriana* Balf.	0.43	0.4
108	Lodgepole pine	*Pinus contorta* Douglas ex Louden	0.38	0.38
109	Coulter pine	*Pinus coulteri* D. Don	0.43	0.4
113	Limber pine	*Pinus flexilis* James	0.37	0.5
116	Jeffrey pine	*Pinus jeffreyi* Grev. & Balf.	0.37	0.36
117	Sugar pine	*Pinus lambertiana* Dougl.	0.34	0.35
119	Western white pine	*Pinus monticola* Dougl. ex D. Don	0.36	0.47
120	Bishop pine	*Pinus muricata* D. Don	0.45	0.45
122	Ponderosa pine	*Pinus ponderosa* P. & C. Lawson	0.38	0.35
124	Monterey pine	*Pinus radiata* D. Don	0.4	0.4
127	Gray or California foothill pine	*Pinus sabiniana* Douglas ex Douglas	0.4	0.4
130	Scotch pine	*Pinus sylvestris* L.	0.43	0.4
133	Singleleaf pinyon	*Pinus monophylla* Torr. & Frém.	0.43	0.4
137	Washoe pine	*Pinus washoensis* H. Mason & Stockw.	0.43	0.4
201	Bigcone Douglas-fir	*Pseudotsuga macrocarpa* (Vasey) Mayr	0.45	0.44
202	Douglas-fir	*Pseudotsuga menziesii* (Mirb.) Franco	0.45	0.44

Table 5—Specific gravity for major tree species wood and bark (continued)

FIA code	Common name	Scientific name	Wood-specific gravity	Bark-specific gravity
211	Redwood	*Sequoia sempervirens* (Lamb. ex D. Don) Endl.	0.36	0.43
212	Giant sequoia	*Sequoiadendron giganteum* (Lindl.) J. Buchholz	0.34	0.34
231	Pacific yew	*Taxus brevifolia* Nutt.	0.6	0.59
242	Western redcedar	*Thuja plicata* Donn ex D. Don	0.31	0.37
251	California torreya (nutmeg)	*Torreya californica* Torr.	0.41	0.42
263	Western hemlock	*Tsuga heterophylla* (Raf.) Sarg.	0.42	0.5
264	Mountain hemlock	*Tsuga mertensiana* (Bong.) Carr.	0.42	0.41
312	Bigleaf maple	*Acer macrophyllum* Pursh	0.44	0.48
313	Boxelder	*Acer negundo* L.	0.42	0.5
321	Rocky Mountain maple	*Acer glabrum* Torr.	0.47	0.53
322	Bigtooth maple	*Acer grandidentatum* Nutt.	0.47	0.53
330	Buckeye, horsechestnut spp.	*Aesculus* spp.	0.33	0.5
333	California buckeye	*Aesculus californica* (Spach) Nutt.	0.33	0.5
341	Tree of heaven (Ailanthus)	*Ailanthus altissima* (Mill.) Swingle	0.46	0.45
351	Red alder	*Alnus rubra* Bong.	0.37	0.56
352	White alder	*Alnus rhombifolia* Nutt.	0.37	0.56
361	Pacific madrone	*Arbutus menziesii* Pursh	0.58	0.6
374	Water birch	*Betula occidentalis* Hook.	0.51	0.58
375	Paper birch	*Betula papyrifera* Marsh.	0.48	0.56
431	Giant chinkapin, golden chinkapin	*Chrysolepis chrysophylla* (Dougl. ex Hook.) Hjelmqvist	0.42	0.42
475	Curlleaf mountain-mahogany	*Cercocarpus ledifolius* Nutt.	0.52	0.53
492	Pacific dogwood	*Cornus nuttallii* Audubon ex Torr. & Gray	0.58	0.58
500	Hawthorn spp.	*Crataegus* spp.	0.52	0.53
510	Eucalyptus spp.	*Eucalyptus fruticetorum* F. Muell.	0.52	0.53
511	Tasmanian bluegum	*Eucalyptus globules* Labill.	0.52	0.53
540	Ash spp.	*Fraxinus* spp.	0.51	0.46
542	Oregon ash	*Fraxinus latifolia* Benth.	0.5	0.5
591	Holly	*Ilex* spp.	0.5	0.5
600	Walnut spp.	*Juglans* spp.	0.44	0.37
603	Northern California black walnut	*Juglans hindsii* (Jeps.) Jeps. ex R.E. Sm.	0.44	0.37
631	Tanoak	*Lithocarpus densiflorus* (Hook. & Arn.) Rehd.	0.58	0.62
660	Apple spp.	*Malus* spp.	0.61	0.5
730	California sycamore	*Platanus racemosa* Nutt.	0.46	0.6
740	Cottonwood and poplar	*Populus* spp.	0.35	0.46
741	Balsam poplar	*Populus balsamifera* L.	0.31	0.5
742	Eastern cottonwood	*Populus deltoides* Bartram ex Marsh.	0.37	0.38
745	Plains cottonwood	*Populus deltoides* Bartram ex Marsh. ssp. *monilifera* (Aiton) Eckenwalder	0.35	0.46
746	Quaking aspen	*Populus tremuloides* Michx.	0.35	0.5
747	Black cottonwood	*Populus balsamifera* L. ssp. *trichocarpa* (Torr. & A. Gray ex Hook.) Brayshaw	0.31	0.4
748	Fremont cottonwood	*Populus fremontii* S. Watson	0.41	0.41

Table 5—Specific gravity for major tree species wood and bark (continued)

FIA code	Common name	Scientific name	Wood-specific gravity	Bark-specific gravity
755	Mesquite	*Prosopis* spp.	0.78	0.65
756	Honey mesquite	*Prosopis glandulosa* var. *torreyana* (L.D. Benson) M.C. Johnst.	0.78	0.65
758	Screwbean mesquite	*Prosopis pubescens* Benth.	0.78	0.65
760	Cherry and plum	*Prunus* spp.	0.47	0.63
763	Chokecherry	*Prunus virginiana* L.	0.47	0.63
768	Bitter cherry	*Prunus emarginata* (Dougl. ex Hook.) D. Dietr.	0.47	0.63
800	Oak	*Quercus* spp.	0.59	0.58
801	California live oak	*Quercus agrifolia* Née	0.59	0.58
805	Canyon live oak	*Quercus chrysolepis* Liebm.	0.7	0.64
807	Blue oak	*Quercus douglasii* Hook. & Arn.	0.59	0.58
810	Emory oak	*Quercus emoryi* Torr.	0.59	0.58
811	Engelmann oak	*Quercus engelmannii* Greene	0.59	0.58
815	Oregon white oak	*Quercus garryana* Dougl. ex Hook.	0.64	0.63
818	California black oak	*Quercus kelloggii* Newberry	0.51	0.45
821	California white oak	*Quercus lobata* Née	0.55	0.55
839	Interior live oak	*Quercus wislizeni* A. DC.	0.59	0.58
901	Black locust	*Robinia pseudoacacia* L.	0.66	0.29
920	Willow	*Salix* spp.	0.36	0.5
922	Black willow	*Salix nigra* Marsh.	0.36	0.5
926	Balsam willow	*Salix pyrifolia* Andersson	0.36	0.5
928	Scouler's willow	*Salix scouleriana* Barratt ex Hook.	0.36	0.5
981	California-laurel	*Umbellularia californica* (Hook. & Arn.) Nutt.	0.51	0.55
990	Desert ironwood	*Olneya tesota* Barratt ex Hook.	0.52	0.53
998	Unknown hardwood	Unknown	0.52	0.53
999	Other or unknown live tree	Unknown	0.52	0.53

Note: Tree species code (SPP) 298 and 326 are not listed in the table (Miles and Smith 2009) and the specific gravities from similar tree species were applied.

Sources: Miles and Smith 2009. Missing species assigned specific gravity with similar species.